to the world, for giving me space to grow,
and to all of my friends and family that
witnessed this journey with me

words from a

wayward childhood

It is okay to stray from your roots,
Sometimes the apple will fall far from its tree,
But that only means,
You are forging the way
For a variety of others
To grow.

07.20.18.

Balance

There is something 'bout the
Summer's end,
The warmth and shine are hers to lend,
A sweetest goodbye
To this dear friend,
As your melancholy of woe
Will soothe and mend
Her swaying soul,
The birds instead sing their songs of sighing,
Even the clouds do comprehend, and the weeds
buckle under
Great gusts of many winds,
The trees give up their leaves
To dying,
And the breeze howls in despair,
The air is thick with hesitation,
As the plants cease their vying,
The lukewarm sun's tired breaths resound,
And the moon adorns its shade of clouds-
As if no longer trying

A life of balance will she show
To all of those
That come and go,
If she had not sang
Such bittersweet sonnet-
The coexistence,
The yin and yang,
An even scale of

Ebullience and tribulation,
There would be no need
For triumph or congratulation.

08.15.18.

Girlhood

Girlish crushes, youthful obsessions,
Slumber parties, secret confessions,
Staying up late,
Laughing beneath
The oversized covers,
Dreaming about
Our future lovers;
Consolation in the form
Of stupid jokes,
Giggling 'til we almost choke,
Counting the years
We've known each other,
Toasting with cheers,
Annoying your brother;
Homemade movies,
Scavenging the mall,
Watching vlogs,
And loving them all,

Growing up, driving,
Whining about class,
Makeup, thriving,
Hoping we'll pass;
This is the flashback
Of a lifelong friend,
To whom my friendship
Will never end.

10.02.18.

Tsunami

Do not settle
To simply make waves
When you can
Be the whole
Tsunami
Itself.

08.14.18.

Little Bird

They tell you to go out and fly
-They make you jump-
But ask them how to flap your wings,
They give no reply

Oh, little bird,
They tell you where you have to fly,
But to land where you'd like,
Still, when you go to rest your wings,
It is not to their delight

So, you flap on and on,
Day to night,
Wondering where to cease your flight,
And when you finally come to land,
You realize
It's the same ground
On which you came from,
Where you now stand.

04.14.18.

Cauterized

There is an aching so deep,
So pure,
So genuine,
It reaches down to my core,
And tears at my seams.
Carefully though, it comforts me,
While it rips me,
Piece by piece,
With a longing,
An internal uproar
That I cannot control,
The embers of a fire
That refuses to be
Put out,
This sea of emotion
Which ceases to tire,
And the missing you
That seems to shout,
With only a whisper- no doubt

05.13.18.

Fireflies

Free into the night sky,
The glittering bodies arise,
Only at dusk can you see their flight,
Their glittering trace, a perfect alibi

Their luminescence is spreading
Like a lovely disease,
A natural, miniscule, display of fireworks
For the trained eye to see,
Undoubtedly, their silent presence somehow
Makes the world complete
In the midst of the clinging summer heat

The children, they are mystified by their burning
beams,
As they try to capture, the dew of twilight swaddling
their feet,
And the fireflies, they recede into the cove of the pine
trees,
Here, one can only see them through the
art of believing

06.29.18.

Insecurities

How can one person
Feel so uncomfortable
In their own skin?
Like it wasn't made to you,
Like you've made a mistake
Over something you cannot control
Your love for others
Must first be extended
Toward yourself,
Before it can have meaning
With anyone else

05.26.18.

He, and the Golden Moments of Summer

And on the days where the sky
Is that bright pink and orange chiffon
Of a watercolor painting,
I'll think of you,
And the tremendous layers of my own fabric,
Ones that you taught me-
Ones that I never knew

07.15.18.

Moonlight

Under the pale moonlight,
This same moonlight
In which our lips first touched,
There was a sense of hope,
A sense of wonder,
A touch of pure euphoria-
A feeling I have never felt before,
A feeling I will never feel again, or so I thought,
And yet here we lie once more,
Under this pale moonlight,
Endless stars in our sight
Though, we don't see the stars, do we?
We only see each other's eyes,
Our souls, connected in a way we never thought
possible,
This same feeling comes back to me,
As it does every time I look at you,
It's under this pale moonlight
I realize,
Time after time,
Happiness exists not,
Unless you are by my side

a poem by E.K.
07.17.18.

Lose Someone

Until you lose someone you love
Permanently
Never tell me
You cannot handle this,
Because if I made it through,
There's nothing you can't do

03.16.18.

Mothers

Join the angels,
You pure soul.
Dwell with the clouds of peace,
And their gentle glow.
Spread your wings, and
Adorn your precious fleece
Of morality.
For you were always
The unseen force,
To help others graciously
In time of need.
But, as you were struggling
To save the light of your soul,
The Earth decided that it did not deserve
Such an outflow
Of purity,
And unwavering charity
As you endow.

08.05.18.

The Clouds

Yes, my mind may dwell
Somewhere out in the clouds,
But do not underestimate,
Or attempt to look past,
Because these clouds are meant to
Conceal a storm,
And I will not be afraid
To strike you down.

07.28.18.

Improvement

Don't tell me
I'm not good enough,
If you refuse to help me improve,
Because,
As far as I'm concerned,
The only thing stopping me
Is you.

03.18.18.

100 Flowers

One hundred flowers in a field,
All the same for one to yield,
Some damaged,
Broken by the wind and sun,
Another, a prominent,
Perfect one
Further and further away you stray,
Each one becoming
Even more the same,
But if you look at each intricate design
Individually,
Every one is a little more unique
Than they seem

04.20.18.

Ocean Side

You ran with me to the ocean tide,
The sand gnawing every tan line,
We jumped waves 'til the sun rose high,
I could not swim,
But you were here, always
By my side.
Specks of purple, black, gold- treasures to this
Young heart of mine,
I now hold this peace of us
Buried deep inside,
A place where this moment
Will forever reside.
I long to rewind
To a time so sublime,
When the sun was yours,
And the sea was mine.

09.23.18.

Pretty Girl

You look at the world
Like you're looking at a field
Of withered grass
In the springtime,
But, pretty girl,
If you look at little closer,
You'll see, that you are the withered grass
Among people most sublime

04.27.18.

The Atmosphere

As tall as a mountain,
                As vast as the oxygen in the atmosphere
                                Around us,
                        But still, you crush me underfoot.
                If only you could see
That it serves to give me purpose.

                                04.29.18.

Well It's Not the Sky's Fault

I am sick with the anticipation of knowing,
That, due to an emotional miscalculation,
I have ruined a friendship in its mediocrity,
But I was hurt,
Distressed in being taken nonchalantly

It is like finding out that the grass never cared about
me,
Until I tread upon its slender sprouts,
And it never knew I existed,
Did not recognize it, at least,
Until I left my house.
I plucked a blade of its skin,
And let it blow freely through the wind-
To see which way it would fly,
And once I found that it had abandoned me,
I ridiculed the ground, and cursed up at the sky,
Though I knew it was not at fault

But the sky called back to me anyway,
And told me that I did not need the grass,
Not even a little, not even at all,
It was then that I realized,
Well, the grass didn't need me either,

The truth is,
While we don't need each other to survive,
We can still grow together,
Live,
Thrive

06.21.18.

Sunrise

I would rather self-destruct
          Than cause an explosion,

          But every dark time,
Gives way to the horizon

04.29.18.

Grounding

The strike of a match
One after another,
Combusting, smoking,
Searing together,
Ignites a forest fire in my mind,
Immune to all extinguishing.
Even the rain of my
Precipitating tears cannot
Quench the smoldering heat
Of negativity.
The hate that I torch my mind in,
I cannot control it,
But to see you through the smoke
Is my only grounding to reality.

08.19.18.

Cobalt Sky

Rise to meet the cobalt sky,
A different perspective for
You and I,
A wish on a cloud,
And the whisper of summer,
A kiss
From the sun,
And the dragonfly's flutter.

08.20.18.

She was the
Night Sky
And you were her sweet
Observatory

08.13.18.

A Certain Type of Cancer

How does it feel,
After everything you've done,
For your own flesh and blood
To turn its back on you?
For your own cells
To multiply indefinitely,
Like the lies you've told,
The secrets you've kept,
The things that you've stolen away
From those
That were not yours to take.
Your entire being is corrupted
By the own familiarity,
The intrusion of yourself.
Your core is rotting
With the self-destruction
That started with your own
Purposeful mistakes,
The day you began focusing
On the superficial
Is the day

That you began losing yourself
Completely.
You are unrecognizable
Even to yourself,
And it will not
Stop growing.

06.01.18.

The First Night

Loving you was like opening a bottle of champagne-
The uncertainty of your first open bottle,
The anticipation of what the initial 'pop' would bring,
The vivid explosion of your imagination
In sync with that of the cork,
And then, the prize:
The free flowing, vibration of the bittersweet liquid
itself,
The burning sensation as it hits your tongue
And you cough in surprise,
As its warm tentacles of bubbly delight trickle through
your chest
And bring a gentle heat to your whole body,
The touching of our lips for the first time,
Under those twinkling stars, and the prickling grass
Against our skin,
Which inspired the heat,
The magnetic touch of our hands,
Awakening every nerve, every cell that was graced by
our fingertips

And it was the knowingness
That this was the start of a thrill,
A spark of pure destiny itself,
That made this first night
Electrifying.

06.21.18.

Overgrown

And when I return to the softball field,
It is overgrown with the dandelions of my youth,
And the vines of my childhood,
They make me remember what it feels like
To grow up
All over again,
Just as they did,
But, I realize
Like these plants,
I am not perennial,
I had my turn on this field,
And now it belongs to them,
They feed on the fountain of my memories,
But are not afraid to shower me in them
When I return

07.19.18.

The Small Things

Your simplicity,
It is eye opening;
A beauty that is strange
To this Earth-
Contentment in the
Small things,
A quality not often learnt.

08.20.18.

Constellation

I could make a constellation out of your eyes
When you look at me,
When we met,
It was like beholding the ageless stars
In their ancient sky.
We summoned their supernovas
With our lips
For the first time,
And now we watch them shoot from heaven,
In our honor,
On this very night.

08.02.18.

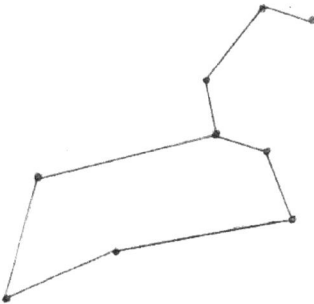

Show me your fangs and I'll show you mine

Stay away, you blood sucking apparition,
Flee!
Before I get the urge to destroy you,
As you did me,
I see your face in strangers,
And it makes me appall them,
I hope your soul is blackened
By the gore of your transgressions,
And your conscience is torn
Like my fragile skin,
As some sort of retribution
Because, I was innocent,
I deserved more than your veiled malevolence,
I was seeking a friend,
But god knows all I found was your dark eminence,
Masked in helplessness,
Vying for attention,
Anywhere you could find it,
But you found me,
A bright-eyed adolescent,
Filled with every single right intention,
And you used me,
You misused me
And my affection.

Show me your fangs,
You master of deception!
You broke me down,
And when you smelled blood
I saw your true intentions,
Little did you know
I am immune to your venom,
And your true identity
Will never delude me
Again.

08.04.18.

Heroine's Feat

The road outstretched before me
Beckons
With the names of streets
Unknown
And the land where strange fruits
Grow
It is enticing me with its newfound
Heat
And remnants of past
Snows
Its triumphant chorus of unity
Resounds
Buried deep below the
Underground
It calls to me from mountain's
Peak
From valleys
Wide
And oceans
Deep
It litters me with dandelion
Seeds
And natural treasures not yet
Found
If only I was not restrained in this deep

Sleep
Slumbering, stuck throughout reality's
Dream
I could have felt Earth's heart
Pound
The steady rhythm of adventure's
Beat
But here I am, awoken to this
Sound,
Never too late for my heroine's
Feat.

08.11.18.

Between Summer and Fall

My favorite season is not a season at all,
It is the cusp between summer and fall,
Where the trees turn candy apple blends,
And all of nature sighs in deliberation
Of what was, and what could be,
A gestation of warm to cold,
Dancing between the new and old,
This cusp between summer and fall
Is not a season, not even a little, not even at all!

09.30.18.

Checkpoints

The checkpoints in life
So victoriously achieved by others
Seem so empty to me,
A piece of my conquest has been stolen,
Indefinitely,
So that there is this a pinhole
Where my pride should be,
A pinhole gaping with grief
In my eyes,
And its impact is the size
Of a crater, to the
Moon of my heart.

08.16.18.

For Sale

We were broken and dysfunctional, this house was
once a dream for a girl in my past life and her mother,
here they grew and flourished and thrived until she
withered and died, and I was left here to find the
strength to grow back out of the garden among
thorns and rocks that wanted to see me fail, but
I kept going.
My blood, sweat, tears, sleepless nights, endless
fights, and so many prosperous years reside here on
this real estate property. Because yes, yes! It is real to
me, and saying goodbye to so many memories seems
preposterous at best. This is the remnant of a
childhood finally grown, rooted in heartache, joy,
pain, freedom, angst, uncertainty, and all of the
things that molded me. So let me just say-
take care of it as it took care of me, a home is meant
for struggles, life, and growing, so cherish it
throughout all it may bring you, and remember that
there is still a past me somewhere in these grounds,
and she will stay there, never to be found, in the
garden flourishing once more.

09.03.18.

Content

There is a girl
With eyes as wide as the space
She beholds,
Whirling, her hair engulfs her
As her face
Fades into the world,
The vibrations of the music
That is her soul
Reverberates off her skin,
With the collision of emotions,
A frequency
Exclusively her own,
And the whole of her being-
She is connected to the
Metaphysics
Of everything

06.15.18.

String Art

Let me leave my world behind,
The small pinhead of a home,
To my string art map,
One day it will be covered
In the worlds of places I've roamed,
Each one collecting
A piece of my soul,
While sowing me up
Each stitch to a whole,
Until I am embroidered
With my voyages of
Places unknown,
In cities of gold,
And foreign roots grown,
Through stories untold-
My ventures, the mold
Of my string art life,
Cultured and primed
In every pinhole.

09.13.18.

words of
a wandering soul

{They Don't Deserve Us}

We are goddesses
In a world of no religion,
One that promises
Peace and kindness,
Happiness and freedom,
To those that cannot recompense,
And rejection
To all those most genuine

05.06.18

A Plea for Self-Love

You can cover it in primer
And paint it white,
But you are going to have to face the music,
That the writing is on the wall,
The song is engraved in the heart of its people,
And will stay there,
Buried deep

If you take a torch to it,
If you make it fall,
It is still known
To all those
That were graced with its message,
This writing on the wall-
That you can't change yourself
To make others fond of you,
Dressing up the outside
Will only make the words glow brighter,

Be true to who you are,
Because you are the only one
That needs you

04.03.18.

Midnight Thoughts

I may forgive, somehow,
But I will never trust you.

(because you stole my words
and twisted them into spiraled lies
you took my choice away
in my helpless state
so tell me. what the hell else
am I supposed to do?)

07.17.18.

Romanticize Living

Why are roses only infamous
For wilting?
Is their life not worth writing?
Does their mid-bloom health
Seem unworthy of adoring?
Is their pollen undeserving
Of creative musing?

Do not appreciate life after death,
But rather romanticize living
At its fullest,
And blooming in
Its finest.

09.01.18.

Overwhelmed

My mind is starved the ammunition of my own
thoughts,
A solitary confinement that I once called home
Is now bursting at the brim-
Feelings that are not my own,
Tick, drop, trickle, tock
My cup has overflowed.

09.25.18.

~A Letter to Everyone~

The hardest thing to come to terms with,
Is wanting someone to care so much,
That your put their wellbeing
Before your own,
Hoping that, someday, they might notice,
But you end up alone

I am your biggest fan,
It is not reciprocated,
That's okay,
Because I am here
Only to give,
Not to be appreciated

05.07.18.

Writer's Folly

Winding words and binding tales,
Oceans rough and wind filled sails,
The air of adventure through your ink,
Grows more enchanted in each thought you think.
The writer's folly is in being contained,
What a vile travesty- creativity restrained!
When you unbind your mind
From the stigmas of time,
A wonderful chaos is yours to find,
In the sweet embrace of word and rhyme

09.20.18.

Permanent

There are no definite states of being
In a world that cannot grasp
A swaying soul,
You slip through its fingertips
In desperation,
Time and time again,
Dying,
Only to be born
Into the next phase,
While constantly longing
To rest
In a universe of your own.

09.27.18.

Love is Not blind

If love is blind, I want none of it,
If love can hurt you, hit you,
Get away with it,
Then what of it?
I want a love
I can see right through,
A piece of paper, candle side,
Without burning,
Transparent, bulletproof glass,
That neither shatters,
Nor cowers
In the light of
The midday sun.

09.27.18.

They call me your clone,
And that's incredible
Because your face deserved
To grace this Earth
For much longer than it did

07.21.18.

Flowers of a Fresh Grave

The air is thick
With the ominous stench of despair,
A terrible thing has happened here,
A lost soul, fragile and scared,
I could sense it to
The ends of my fingertips,
Even through the mask of fresh air,
My heart, sinking with
The weight of so many others broken,
It has pressed upon mine,
As the soul cultured by flowers
Of a fresh grave
Is spread throughout the land,
It is a tragic shame-
Death
Had once again outstretched its hand,
And breathed its fatal breath
Upon an innocent soul once more,
Always will it be unjust,
Always this will I implore.

08.19.18.

Pollution

Your conscience is fleeting
As the remnants of a toxic breath
Striking cold air,
It disperses
As each tiny particle,
With no final destination,
Concealed within the solace
Of those around it

But my dreams,
They guide me,
As the smoke of
A burning cigarette,
Whose pollution goes to meet
The stars above,
Concentrated among the force field
Of Earth,
Contaminating every element
In its path

I am infectious,
I am everywhere, and
I am nowhere at the same time,
But somehow, my pollutant
Shows more promise
Than any trace of you
I could have inhaled,
Believing in clean air

08.22.18.

Inconsistencies

I am the summer breeze
That comes to quench the scorching heat
Of its misery,
I am the pestilence
In times of solitude,
When there is no need for
Such a Destruction
As I ensue,
I am longed for
At the brunt of midday,
When the sun reaches its full strength,
And detested most
When the last of light is erased
From the sky,
I am the nameless ghost,
A 'something' from a past life
That not even nature
Can dignify

05.07.18.

Today I Leap

I am capable of much more
Than this box you've put me in,
Maybe if you took a good look at my container,
You would find that it can no longer hold me,
You cannot win.

it will not contain her

I've surrendered to those walls too many times,
But not today,
For today I leap, tomorrow I fly

07.17.18.

The Smoldering Inquisition

Your hatred is focused on me,
For my variety of "infidelities".
I can feel the warmth radiate
From such a fire in your chest,
How dare I be different?
My sexuality
Should not be the kindling
For your fire of rage,
Nor the stage
For your
Crusade of homophobia.
But you won't change.
So take that damn spark, you hypocrite,
And burn me at the stake.

07.21.18.

[Anthem of Anxiety]

I want to scream
Until the wildfire
Of anger in my chest ceases,
Until this anxiety releases
Its goddamn iron grip on me
Because -

I know I am strong
And capable
Of being my own song,
Marching to my own beat,
I am the conductor,
I am the leader,

I am constantly lost
Searching within myself
For the power to contain
My own fire,
But I am far too withered
By the salt of my bitter tears,
Merely igniting the pain
And stoking the flame.

08.23.18.

Familial Oppression

You are forever burdened
By the sinking weight
Of your family,
For they do not realize what
A beautiful soul
You truly are,
And if you do not
Use yourself
As your own flotation device,
They will drown you
In their own expectations,
And corrode all of the individuality
And love
That even you
Have not yet discovered.

08.13.18.

Something, or a big nothing

Climbing
Is an endless flight of stairs,
You reach one landing
And are back where you've started
Four years ago,
You are persistently patient,
The model of endurance,
So shouldn't you deserve the best?
No,
You signed up for all of it,
The good, the awful, the heartlessness,
The kind, the broken.
But you've been misused,
And in that misuse
You'll find that she's fallen off
Your staircase-
A downward tumble,
One that she cannot wake up from,
Flashes of color
In her pitiful spirals:
Gray, the numbness,
Black, the emptiness,
White, the possibilities,

A big, gigantic nothingness
-But the funny part is
This is all speculation,
Based on my own state
Of falling.

06.07.18.

Reconstruction

Your words,
They struck me like a brick,
If only I had enough mortar
To seal them up
With the rest,
Maybe someday I could build a wall high enough
That I'll no longer get hit

07.18.18.

Dull Ache of Uselessness

Sometimes my heart bleeds,
Longing to give a piece
Of itself
To heal someone else.
So I use the strength
Of some imaginary willpower,
Waiting to be defeated,
And my insides wrench
With the dull throb of uselessness,
As I lie here,
Moment by moment fleeting,
Wishing the existence of magic
Amidst my insides,
As this heart keeps beating-
A prognosis so very tragic.
But maybe,
Maybe healing does exist,
In its own form of sorcery,
Where it is least expected.

08.05.18.

When the Willow Breathes

The cry of the willow,
With her gleaming, tangled roots,
Complicated in every tangible direction,
Unfeigned by the ones that came before her,
Or the birds that peck at her bark,
Menacingly attempting to rot her core

To make her as black
As the feathers they inherited
From their own,
Filled with the sorrows of their journeys,
The fruitlessness of their perils,
The wealth of their generations

They are awaiting the fall
Of the willow,
So pure,
So cultured,
So earthly,
Because they know

When the willow releases her seeds,
Filled with the knowledge and power,
Only originating from the ground itself-

When she spills her core of reason
And morality,
When she breathes life
Into the soul of the Earth,
The sky will fall,
And the birds will bow to her
Ancient Roots,
She will breathe,
And the whole world will go silent
Awaiting her words,
Which will bleed into
Every foundation
That the world was built upon

03.24.18.

Self-Sufficiency at its ~~Best~~ Worst

I would like to wrench the power
From the evil penmanship
Of society,
The death grip
Brainwashing its citizens
Into its own standards:
That monetary value
Is more vital
Than morality,
This belief that
We all must be self-sufficient,
That we should take only what we need,
With no regard for the impact
It has on others,
This underlying belief
That selfishness
And cruelty will get you farther
Than love and kindness,
Because when it comes down to it,
No government,
No system,
No program,
Is going to save you,

It is we
That must be there
To save each other

06.19.18.

The Orchids

They whisper to me
With such a solemn secret,
One that cannot be discovered
By those of unworthy ears,
Their tender buds,
All aligned, connected by a common life force
They are so sweet, so raw,
Their delicate drapery accents the world
Around them,
And their blooming-
Their blooming is an eruption
Of disbelief,
A rare oddity to be interpreted by the eyes,
They look so familiar,
Yet, each so inconceivably different,
What do they whisper? And why to me?
It may not be such a secret after all,
Are you worthy?

They tell me not to trust the gardener,
For the gardener is meant to care for them,
But the only caring that he does
Is attempt to fill their gentle veins
With poison,
And if these irreplaceable little saplings

Learn to accept the toxin,

Then the gardener has won,

But if they reject his duplicitous scheme,

They are considered worthless,

And no longer fit to be seen

You see, the gardener's poison is

monotony,

uniformity,

and control,

There is no room for different,

Not even space to grow,

The orchids are calling to you now,

Warning you about the temptation

That awaits with such a vile man,

Oh, Bleeding Heart,

Save yourself,

It may not be easy this way

But, grow, bloom, prosper

As magnificently as such a treasure can

06.19.18.

Women

The way we come together in alliance- no matter shape, size, color, class. Those of us who say "me too" and continue seeing love in the mirror, there is nothing stronger. Those who find the courage to embrace others, even after every strike of grief tells them not to, you are my heroine. When the world shows us injustice, we do not sit on the sidelines of battle. We bear our armor, we bleed, we weep, we fight, we *keep fighting*. We will continue fighting until our onlookers see our scars and are afraid. Even then, we will press on, until those who dare disrespect us have eyes wide enough to swallow them whole. Until the very Earth expands, and collapses into itself once more. Until the universe turns itself inside out at the sight of us. We will not back down until we have flipped this world onto its head, and have taught it how to walk on its fingertips.

09.18.18.

Begin Again

You've fought the most
Gruesome of battles
And your ferocity
Is most admirable,
But sometime, you must
Learn to stop
Falling on your own sword,
It is a blade meant for others,
Wash yourself
In your fountain of restoration
And begin again.

09.06.18.

Inspiration

A figure dripping
With
The angst of creativity,
The pain of musings,
The raw emotional time stamps
That compose life itself.
These are the collection
Of such wonders
That can never be
Extinguished.

08.14.18.

Is my mirror offending you?

Sometimes you have to be obsessed with yourself
-So utterly infatuated, because-
Baby, self-worth is the most attractive form of
romance

07.16.18.

Survive

Held me down,
You clenched my throat,
Slapped my face,
And watched me choke,
Broke my heart,
And saw me writhe,
All my winces,
You denied.
Thrust yourself into
My life,
Wound your hand,
I watched you strike,
An innocent girl was I that day,
Until you took my choice away.

09.29.19.

When the lines are blurred, write harder

The celestial fight between black and white
Is an eternal tug of war,
The power falls to you
To choose which side of the rope
Will be pushed over precipice's edge,
You, the poet,
Must decide which evil will consume your soul,
If either,
Because, whether black or white prevail,
Gray still possesses the words of your
Spellbound notebook.
Each opponent to this war
Has its darkness,
As does each side to your poems,
They are one in the same-
A double-edged blade,
And even worse,
A blade with the power to choose,
Or a blade with the embers of divergence.

08.06.18.

-Child's Play-

You.
You are the boy
That made my screams echo
Across every dimension
Of my subconscious,

You are a child,
But a child capable of more damage
Than you have ever known
For you,
The fragile heart of the little girl
You *destroyed*
Was just a game
-Child's Play-

But if I had the chance to stand up,
Right to that face,
The face that haunted me in the same shadows
Of my mind
All of these years,
I would say *thank you,*
Because without you,
I would've never known such pain,
This pain that broke me
Scar after year after scar

Once I had died for a while,
I realized that no one,
No.One.
Has.the.power.
To.make.me.feel.
So worthless,
Damaged,
Or broken,
As you had done
For all that time

So *thank you,*
Thank you for ruining me,
Still to this day,
I feel the remnants
Of your damned razor blades,
Your sick little game,
But, lucky for this world,
I have repaired the havoc
You have reaped on that little girl,
And gave her a new passion,
One that no longer revolves around *you,*
It is unquenchable,
All due to your little games,
How does it feel now?
-Child's Play-

07.17.18.

Reincarnate

I wish
I could live
A thousand lives
To discover every inch
Of my own wondrous being
But then again
Maybe I will

08.13.18.

If nothing else-
Be happy
For happiness is the only catalyst
That can make you forget
A lifetime of suffering
If only
For a moment
I can assure you
It is worth every sentiment

-If nothing else
07.18.18.

The Musical Genius

Your mind is a symphony
Of passion
And a tune of creativity,
There are no right or wrong notes
To your composition,
Only allure,
Harmony,
And tasteful contemplation.

The notes, they swirl around you
In a typhoon of wonderful possibilities,
Waiting on your artistic ingenuity
To transform them
Into a work of pure beauty.

07.21.18.

Loyalty

Is a hungering love
Which craves the basic forms
Of retaliation
It is forever destined
To be malnourished
Even still, forgotten.

08.17.18.

A compilation of beautiful disasters:

- The way the leaves take flight through the strongest breeze
- The way the wind blows freely, with no regard to appease
- The way the sun beats down, with no reverence to burning
- The way the moon steals her light, with no desire to please
- The way the fish swim on, through the thick of the reef
- The way the tornado destroys, even the most frivolous of dreams
- The way the water gnaws against the shore for her seas
- The way the desert storm destroys with sandy ease
- The way a flower blooms and releases her seeds
- The way a creature survives in her endangered species
- The way I'll live on, when my heart ceases to beat

08.28.18.

Congratulations

And at the end of the night,
When all of the searing lights
Of my few moments of fame have come to an end,
I realize that I cannot receive a "congratulations"
From the one that matters most,
And I cannot comprehend
The look on her face,
At this very moment,
If she were not out there
Occupying some unimaginable place in space,
Wishing that things were different,
And wondering what life would be like
With her here

06.22.18.

Downpour

To hear the pounding
Of fall's warm droplets,
Is to find peace
In my lost, fraying soul,
I am drowning in the downpour,
As I watch the river grow,
While I am safely ashore,
With my anchor and boat,
Watching these ghosts of me
Choke.

09.26.18.

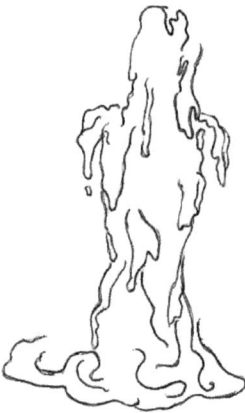

Femininity

Femininity is no hour glass,
It has no definition of class,
The only quality femininity has
Is confidence,
A confidence with no consequence,
It cannot be described superficially,
And assigning it boundaries
Is the formula to fraudulence.
It is not promiscuous,
And it is not synonymous
With the mainstream idea of beauty.
Femininity is predominance,
Predominance of self-image,
And sometimes it must be grown,
Cultured by its beholder,
And loved by none other
Than yourself.

08.04.18.

Thorns

Your body is a blossomed garden,
An intricate cynosure completely your own,
Meaning:
You are the only one
To decide
Who can and cannot yield a flower
From your precious growth.
Do not let your lovely garden get trampled over;
Left to rot.
For if it does,

You have thorns

Hidden beneath
Your vibrance
For a reason.

07.19.18.

I wonder
If the sun ever grows weary
Of lending its radiant beams
To those that have nothing
To offer in return,
Save heartbreak and suffering.

- *I wonder*
08.17.18.

The Deluge

What happened to the world
Where everyone respected each other?
A place where you could feel safe walking down a
street,
Undisturbed,
Knowing that neighbors were as good as brothers.
Why can't we be ourselves
Without being unnerved
From the dangers of being raped, beaten, abused?
Maybe people should stop caring so much about who
you love:
Black, white, Asian, male, female, transgender,
And focus on the roots of this
Societal misuse,
And work together
To make this *difference,*
Something I have never even discovered.

Where is this inordinate place
That I've only heard of,
Where people were kind to strangers, every person,
every race?
But now, I cannot talk to anyone without putting
them in this
Stereotyped container,

Making me so paranoid, even suspicious,
But, "stranger danger",
Right?

America, we can do better,
Foreigners come here,
Not because of the attractions, the sight-seeing, the
citizens, or the weather,
They come here because we've promised
Freedom, safety- a place with no need to waver,
But we rip their families apart,
Treat them like criminals,
We put them in cages,
And we break their hearts,
When all they wanted was refuge
From their physical, emotional, and tyrannical lives-
The magnificent deluge
Of demise
That is their homeland.

We cannot even care for our own,
Those that have fought to protect our lands
End up on the streets,
The ghosts of soldiers, mistreated, damaged, and
beat,
Where is our gratitude for the sacrifices of
Our guardian angels?

They have been deemed obsolete!
They were seen as broken, dysfunctional, poor, and
mangled,
Their mental roots stemming from battle,
Far from detangled!
But here they sit, being ignored,
Begging for change
Outside of closed doors,
Wondering who will uphold
The justice they deserve.

And let's talk about our women
Said to be "fine now",
They have all of their rights, good men, equal jobs,
nice bank accounts,
But what about the women everyday
That go about their lives, being told what to say,
How to dress,
How to act,
So that men won't be tempted
To stalk and attack.
Tell me about the women who are still treated as
objects,
They can never be themselves
They'll just end up a reject
(Because of how they were born),
Tell me about our little girls

That grow up thinking they have to conform

To the rest of the world

-In effort to prevent its dismay-

So they're just hungry

Every single day.

And tell me about all of the dreams

Being disposed of

Because they are just women,

And the *properties of a household*

They have no place in leadership, vital positions, government,

Or so I am told,

America, where is our mercy,

And our respect for life,

With our laziness, our wastefulness, our greed, our strife?

How can we allow preventable habits

To ruin our precious Earth?

We cannot continue to treat our animals

With no dignity or worth,

They cannot speak for themselves or even put up a fight,

And I do not think you'd want them to

For they would condemn us,

And they would be right.

Pure souls of this corrupt nation,

Where is our voice?
It is up to us to start making a difference
And stop ignoring things that do not affect us,
For this is our choice.
The stripes on our flag, so patriotic
Should multiply and combust-
To burn with the abundance of inhumanities that we
inflict,
Our anthem should resound with the voices,
The screams of this country's victims.
And our soil, that we value so much,
Should be drenched in the blood, sweat, and dreams
Of all those that we've ruined,
And all of the promises we haven't kept.
I am not exempt
From this treachery,
But I am a strong believer
That we can all grow together,
And fix- *we must repair*
Our immoral, spiraling, tumultuous
Country in despair.

06.23.18.

It takes a truly lovely mind
To appreciate real beauty,
So darling,

Let them stare.

07.19.18.

Fresh Air

She is a model
Without all the lights,
The cameras,
The fad diets,
The makeup,
Or the fake demeanor.
She is a model
For being unconditionally
Herself,
And she does
Not need her picture
Taken
To be beautiful.

There is something so
Exquisite
About her
Originality,
In its utter simplicity,
That makes the onlookers stare.

She is a muse
Wrapped in artistry,
Rather than chiffon,
And a sweet symphony
Of rarity
To the world's trending songs.
She is a breath of
Fresh air.

08.13.18.

Learning-

Is the sweet epitome of my soul,
While love
Inspires such vital growth.
I have found both in the stanzas:
The poem that is in me,
The poem that is my own.

07.17.18.

My head is filled
With more
Poetry
Than you could lay
Your eyes
Upon in
An entire
Lifetime.

08.11.18.

whimsical
words of fiction

What a curious thing, hope is

Baby blue eyes looking up at the sky,
Ever since birth
Mama told her to fly,
And when she came of age
She would look out to the birds in the night,
"I have no wings", was her reply.

Day and night she watched her mother,
Cook, and clean, and take no lover,
"Go! Go and soar!" her mama told her,
But only in disbelief would her mind hover.

One day she awoke, mama nowhere to be found,
And she turned the whole house upside down,
She walked to the river, to see if she had drowned,
But found her kneeled down,
Mind strewn about the ground,
Not even a trace of a frown,
But still, she pleaded with the sound
Of urgency echoing all around.

And she looked up at the sky,
Once again,
And told her to go out and fly-
Not to worry about the birds in the night,

"But mama, why? Why?" Was her reply.
She took her last breath looking up still at that same
sky,
And her soul, vibrant and full, full of life,
Went up to join the winds in their flight.
And still, the little girl did not believe,
Until she saw the look in her mother's
Motionless eyes.

So she went out and built a basket made of straw,
And strung it with balloons of every color,
Alone, she drifted off
With nothing out there to stop her.
Up, up still she went!
With her contraption of a pauper,
She looked down and saw the house,
The house of her unknown father,
And she looked down and saw herself,
Herself, and her mother!

And she cried out to the passing mountains,
glittered with the twinkling snow,
Pleading, *how had this happened?*
And where was she to go?
She looked down once more to watch the tragic
scene unfold,
And there she saw it:

Her mother kneeling all alone
By the water, a frown as cold and stiff as the snow,
And she looked up at the sky, saw her daughter afloat,
Up! And up! Away from their miserable abode.

She smiled, that one tremendous look,
And gazed toward her daughter,
The daughter she had mistook for a non-believer.
She knew that she would make it,
She could see it in the book,
The book that the sky unfolded,
The book, that damned book,
At which her whole world shook.

And mama wished that she could join her
Out there with the stars,
So, she breathed out her soul,
And it bled through all the pages,
Out into space, and even to Mars!

Her daughter looked up at the sky, and knew what she had to do,
And now, looking down from those colored balloons,
She could only wonder what was real
And what was simply a rune.

07.13.18.

Skyscraper

Gray high rises outline the pavement
With the demeanor of intimidation,
Each equipped with its reputation
Of magnificence,
And its abundance of levels; winding turns,
All an enigma of something other than
Benevolence,
But the look on her face
At the end of each day
As she watches her grand shadow
Diminish its display,
Is the only way one can know
How small she truly is
Without the transformative glow
Of her sunlight.

06.07.18.

The Rebirth

Come with me
Into the overgrown haven
Of the willow trees
Where their sweet symphonies
Of rustling vines
Will caress our days
Until the end of time,
When we emerge, someday,
From their elixir of preservation
And solitude,
We will find a new world,
A vestigial serenity,
Beginning
From the rebirth,
And gentle cleansing
Of the Earth

07.18.18.

Dear Stan

Home! Home!
Where the humans roam,
Day after day while they leave me alone,
And I am wondering, and wandering, and pondering
What I've done to deserve such neglect,
But yet here I sit, and I lick
The same spot on my paw each day,
And I protect,
Oh, I protect their home so well!
I bark at squirrels, and at people-
Anything harmful,
But yet, all I get is rejection,
So, what was a pup to do? I left.
I ran and ran and ran, chasing van after car after van,
There are so many things to see here,
And so many new things to do,
I even ignored the mailman!
I watched birds at the park,
And ate food in the streets,
I left my mark
On every tree,
'Cause god knows they get mad
If I stop every five feet.

When they brought me home for the first time
It was the most elated I've ever felt,
But as you can see from this rhyme
It was the worst card
I could have been dealt.

So here I sit,
Somewhere far, far away,
But somehow, still, these moments grow darker each
day,
Nothing is new anymore,
I must go farther! My mind implores,
So I do,
I ran and ran and ran, chasing van after car after van,
And I sit on a stoop,
Wondering where on Earth I am,
And if they were out there somewhere,
In their monster of a van,
Calling out for their dear, dear Stan.

But here I was, I realized,
Thinking about them more than I thought I would
fantasize,
And I remembered! Oh, I remembered how good life
used to be,
When the kids were still at home, I was just a puppy,
We would play all day long,

And they would laugh, and even sing me songs,
All the walks we used to take,
Sometimes, I would watch as they tried to bake
Those dog snacks for me,
As I pretended to love those awful treats,
I'd watch them squirm while I licked their feet,
And I loved life.

But now, they're all gone,
Their feet, and their laughs, and their treats,
The old man is older than I ever imagined he'd be,
He just sits all day, stares, and watches TV,
And my mom- one day they took her-
She'd fallen on the floor,
They took her away, and I would see her no more.

Here, as I wander, and I wonder, and I ponder
It dawns on me,
It's not their fault!
They, too, have things to see,
Places to run, people to become,
I have made a mistake,
The old man, he needs me,
As much as he needed my mom,
And I was lost, lost as could be!

Where was my home?

The home where *my* humans roam!

They need me more- more than I've ever known,

And I need them too,

I'm not sure where I am anymore,

I am completely alone,

Completely alone, and I must find my home!

I saw my own face,

Plastered on every window, and on every pole,

They care, they really do need me!

So I race, and I leap, and I race,

Until I spot the place-

A grown-over pond and a big oak tree,

The door is shut and the car is gone,

What have I done?

So I wait,

I wait at the front gate

All through the night and up until dawn,

Until I see it, the old, ugly red van,

I leap for joy when I see the old man,

And he falls on his knees, ground against his hands,

Out of the van come the kids, all grown up now, but as fast as they can,

"Stan!"

I've done it, I've found my family,

I've found the old man,

And as we walk, he tells me all the places they've
gone – just looking for me, Stan!
We roam,
Once again, he is happy,
I have done it,
I have found my home,
And really, what a good home it is for me.

07.15.18.

A Subtle Scent

The petrichor of a thousand winds
Knows me by name,
For I have appreciated its
Subtle elegance-
A lovely perfume that is in no way
Tamed by the sun,
Or ruined by the rays
Of an admired rainbow.
I have treasured its scent,
Such a sweet fragrance,
And cleansing aura glow
Have I cherished,
Each time it has
Crossed my senses.

08.09.18.

Consciousness;

I arise from the forest
To an infinite number of paths,
None of them flawless,
I am guided by the wind-
The sun and moon, simply an illusion,
The driving force originating within,
I travel down a path- yes it's dark at times,
Roots erupt from the Earth,
Threatening to ensnare me
In their labyrinths of beautiful deceit,
But I feel it within,
I am drawn to a place
Completely my own,
Shielded from the moon and sun
-The wild-
And I breathe.

05.05.18.

Luminesce

Light in a dark room,
Bride and a stark groom,
Maiden and her forced loom,
Flowers so scarcely bloomed.

Light feathers on a dark bird,
Vast screams, not yet heard,
A magnificent image, black and blurred,
A lovely body, scarred and burned.

Light is the whisper of a terrible tragedy,
Magic, the choice between terror or majesty,
A murder, gallantry or immorality?
What is the similarity between these oddities?
They all have the power to luminesce past their
calamity,
To bring their hidden truths to reality,
In fact, they must

07.15.18.

If Red Was the Only Color

I hear his voice.
The cold, hard, calloused sound
That renders me no choice but to shudder,
And let the sheer terror surround me.
I can see it:
The red radiating through his pores,
Seeping through his skin.
It is the only color he ever sees.
The crimson darkness,
It brings me to my knees.
I fall to this unforgiving floor,
As the glass picture frame shatters
All around me,
Only to remind me of my life,
Destroyed, tattered,
Marred with the cruelty that was once my lover.
I wonder,
How many will it be today?
One, two, three... Eight, nine, ten?
Nine, nine is my lucky number today,
And all I can see is the scarlet of my own
On this unforgiving floor.
But this time,
This time I strike back, one last blow.
Ten.

There are ten displays of cruelty this time,
But the tenth one,
The knockout,
Is finally mine.

07.27.18.

Tranquility

Do not be afraid
As you dance in the garden
Of the fairy lights,
Let your hair
Release its wet droplets
In a cascade down your back,
And your eyes
Absorb the energy of the night.
Your lips will whisper
The tales of the garden
In time's past,
And your hands will graze the flowers,
As the dragonflies bow to your
Tranquility.

Such a dalliance you have,
You and the garden,
Even the river
In which you came from
Is smitten with jealousy
For such a love affair as this.

Her lover once laid down
In this garden.
He was put to rest,

Sworn to return someday
As the redolent bloomings
In the midst of summer.

And she too, was sworn to him,
And laid down by the river,
Letting the water ripple over her;
Letting it transform her.

At the end of each summer escapade,
They are reunited for one sublime
Nightfall.
Where the fairies twinkle, the crickets sing,
And the lovers
Wait to be reborn.
For this one evening,
The river and garden
Will be rejoined
At last.

07.20.18.

Come one, come all to the circus Nationale!

The circus comes to life
With its bold and searing lights,
The makeup and the fights,
The music and strange sights.

It's an entertainment of sorts
Though the artists that contort
Feel more like puppets
Than they do artists.

And the animals
Are so majestic to see!
The children smile in awe
At the tigers, elephants, monkeys,
Yippee!
But I like to wonder if they'd have the same reaction,
If they went backstage,
Before all the action,
To witness these same creatures
In their fraction of a cage,
And their meals in each ration.

The ringleader gives the crowd what they want!
Spreading fun, dubious energy all around.
But after the show, he can only be found

In his mansion behind the fairgrounds
Despising us all.
He is a hypocrite if there ever was,
Still, every magazine is filled with buzz
Of the incredible circus Nationale,
Because, well, glamour only stretches makeup deep
here,
And they only see what he wants them to see.

The circus freaks are so wonderful to witness,
The sight of their bodies, sometimes hard for one to
digest.
But they all line up and pay their fees, plus interest
To see these circus "freaks".
They were told they would never be hired anywhere
else,
Because they were freakish, ugly, some sort of
eyesore,
So they gave up on their dreams,
And settled for a life of show time misery, abused and
tired.

The food is delicious and circus themed!
The monkey-shaped hot dogs and fries go perfectly
With the half-time show
Of elephant vs. donkey!
But look out behind the tents

And you'll see
A landfill of garbage, old and burning
With the stench of hypocrisy.

The clowns are the highlight of the show,
Dozens and dozens of facial expressions and
emotions-
Although, none of them are a true reflection
Into their heart and soul.
No one truly knows who they are
Aside from the props and costumes in their
collection.
Some are evil,
Some are sad,
And some are just too worn down to fake a frown,
But they play their parts,
And they sway the hearts,
Of everyone in that damn audience.
Except me.
I know the truth behind everyone in the performance,
I see past their hot dogs and fries,
Their condiments of lies,
Makeup, and disguise.

I am the acrobat,
And I found myself trapped in this tragic
Circus act.

Not by choice, I might add.
My mother was a tightrope walker,
And as her daughter,
I was taught
That nothing is as it seems.
It's all one big conspiracy,
Some sort of get-rich-quick scheme,
But not for everybody.
Some vigilante catastrophe,
Masqueraded in blasphemy,
Accepted by society,
Even praised harmoniously.
So I do my act,
In anticipation for the day,
Where I can break this pact of treachery
Once the home of the brave
And show the audience that there's evil
Behind every act they see.
And the land of the free

07.23.18.

bizarre, yet strangely appealing

way out there is where i dwell
in some kind of strange outcast realm
where the trees
are blue tuffets
of cotton candy leaves
and the wild sketch of houses are doodles
from their imaginer's notebook
come to life, from a mere outlook
with inhabitants incapable of evil
and letters, all which are equal
the people, they spend their days feeding the pixel
fish at the park
and go fishing for rose-feathered birds at night,
before dark
where i come from,
i can surf gradient skies with my mind
all through the morning
because time,
time doesn't exist here

here, here in this mind
you'll never age, you'll never die
here, when you've nothing left to create
you'll become part of our universe, you and i,
and we'll exist among the dazzling doodles,

among the abstruse animations,
and all of the dreamed imaginations,
as for me, i will never come down
where here, as simple as a melancholy frown
is not to be found
join me, won't you?

07.17.18.

Hidden Tales

Tell me,
What lies beneath the floorboards?
A majority of stories untold,
A manifold of plants to behold?
Or was there once a mighty oak,
Or a stream running through?
Could it be a valley of fresh flowers bloomed?
The ancient ruins of a forgotten land,
The majestic beach of a thousand sands?
A woody paradise of forests far and wide,
A bungalow of pines,
To which fairies and nymphs reside?

Which story do the tales of these floorboards hide?
Is it all or one?
Is it all or none?
Maybe these are the stories I am not meant to find,
Maybe I shall create them using only
My mind.

08.18.18.

Labyrinth of You

I disappear into the night,
Masqueraded by the cryptic sensation of darkness,
I crave a validation
That I will never acquire.
The soft glow of my fierce hunger
Radiates as gently as my dim lantern set afire,
And I search for you
Through the labyrinthine journey of inspirations,
But somehow you are the buried treasure
That I cannot uncover.
The X does not mark your spot, this time,
Because all of the words I could string together
Could never quite chronicle your masterpiece.

07.21.18.

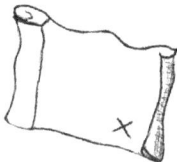

Soliloquy

Write me a soliloquy,
Character in your history
With advanced terminology,
And endless psychology.
The audience will stare
With a damsel as fair as me,
Better than mythology-
But no distress ideology,
And if you try to rescue me
You'll end in despair.
To your damned authority
I am the stubborn mare.

08.12.18.

wild words
        of diverse verse

Writing & Conquesting

Never will I write
Solely to have written, but
For my convictions.

Nor will I top, 'till
My every last ghost is
Vanquished, yes, smitten.

08.10.18.

Azure

Wash me away,
        Azure ocean beads will
Grace my willing skin.

08.08.18.

Champagne + Starry Nights

Get drunk on the night,
                    I promise, you will find no
        Greater emotion.

08.08.18.

Draught

Unconditional;
My love spreads as fog in your
Forest of hatred
Whose trees absorb each raw ounce
Of kindness throughout their draught

08.29.18.

Helpless and scared, you
Had me at the mercy of
Volatile hands.

08.18.18.

Alphabet Soup

I am an alphabet soup
Of longing to make my letters loop
Into something coherent.
But I am also caught, a willing adherent,
Enjoying each sweetly jumbled group.

08.11.18.

But you deserve it, right?

You hurt me
every single day.
Blamed it on
An ailment
That never
Afflicted you.
Lied to my face,
While twisting
Your knife into
My back, said
That you were
The one to be
Pitied, the one
Under attack.
You may not
Have had a disease,
But surely you
Were sick,
Nauseously

Hungering
For whatever
Power you gained
By hurting me,
While I was the
One *falling*,
Withering,
Dying.
And now that
I have made
My recovery
I can only wish
You to get well
Soon,
Before the world
Has its way and
Shows you a
Life far worse
Than what you
Put me through.

08.10.18.

Toxic

Trees will give up their
Leaves in illness, likewise, you
In times of despair

09.30.18.

Inner Child

And in this moment
My inner being has
Fallen to her knees
At the realization
That we can
Never
Regain
This
Version
Of
Us
Again.

09.12.18.

Author's Note

Thank you for your support of my debut collection. I wish to further embark on sister collections to Strange Fruits, and I dearly hope that reading my life in words made each and every one of you feel something. My main purpose in becoming a published author was to share my thoughts with the world, in hopes of connecting all of us through poetry and prose. I have included one final, overarching, poem to complete this collection on the following page.

My Sincerest Thanks,
S.Whitman

Evaporate

I want to disappear
        As the excursions of the rain
                Into soft ground
        After its storm.
I want to revitalize every grain
        Of the precious soil
                I belong to.
I want to evaporate and
        Be renewed all over again-
To span every inch of the world,
        Just by existing
                As a single droplet.

        08.09.18.

www.ingramcontent.com/pod-product-compliance
Lightning Source LLC
La Vergne TN
LVHW041223080426
835508LV00011B/1058